John Haughton

Phil Spector

A short story

JustFiction Edition

Imprint

Any brand names and product names mentioned in this book are subject to trademark, brand or patent protection and are trademarks or registered trademarks of their respective holders. The use of brand names, product names, common names, trade names, product descriptions etc. even without a particular marking in this work is in no way to be construed to mean that such names may be regarded as unrestricted in respect of trademark and brand protection legislation and could thus be used by anyone.

Cover image: www.ingimage.com

Publisher:
JustFiction! Edition
is a trademark of
Dodo Books Indian Ocean Ltd., member of the OmniScriptum S.R.L Publishing group
str. A.Russo 15, of. 61, Chisinau-2068, Republic of Moldova Europe
Printed at: see last page
ISBN: 978-613-7-41904-5

PHIL SPECTOR - A short story by John Haughton

https://www.youtube.com/watch?v=23y7pdefogM

Phil Spector in the early years writing/composing music

He was a rebel in more senses than one and here is his composition-'He's a

Rebel':

https://www.youtube.com/watch?v=jbp1h74-RUs

This is a short story about Phil Spector.   Phil Spector was one of the most

enigmatic people that ever walked on planet earth. In musical terms he was

in this writer's opinion and many musical experts an absolute genius and he

composed music for thousands of songs including for the Beatles and many

other groups. In the course of this short story I hope to give the reader a

comprehensive compendium of his musical works. His music was largely

of the 1960s and I was a youth of the 60s. Some of the songs he composed

featured on everyday radio in the sixties. Without any effort I was immersed

in the music of that period and inevitably the compositions of Phil Spector

which dominated a large part of the popular musical scene of the sixties.

What sparked off the research for this short story was the occasion of the passing of Ronnie Spector who was the lead singer of the Ronettes. in January 2022. Her death marked the end of an era and I decided to delve once again into some of the songs and music that inspired her, and the many groups for whom Phil Spectre composed songs and music. It is an understatement that Ronnie Spectre's marriage to Phil Spector was a very unhappy one and that she was treated very badly by him according to reports. It is a well-known cliché that genius is close to madness and there are those who saw Phil Spector as such a candidate. His last years were particularly sad. He got a life sentence after he was convicted of shooting a woman and died in prison in the year 2020 while carrying out a life sentence for that murder.   In musical terms he was one of the most creative souls. But personality-wise he was not a Mozart or a Sibelius. His personality and attitude come in for severe criticism. This   short story will focus almost entirely on his music and songs and explain to the reader how they were uniquely creative. We will not delve into his personal life and the relationships he had. These are very well documented and can be easily accessed on the internet. One of these was his relationship to Ronnie Spector of the Ronettes. She was married to Phil Spector for a period in what was a very unhappy marriage. I listened to her speech when she and the Ronettes were inducted into the hall of fame. The relationship had been so bitter that Ronnie could not even mention his name in her award speech although in a sense her success could be at least partly attributed to his musical creativity. This is partly explainable by the fact that Spector did not pay the Ronettes for their contributions and they had to go to court and get a judicial decision whereby they got a large settlement for their work. This was opposed by Spector. Ronnie maintained that she was in effect a prisoner for a considerable period during their marriage.

Although this short story will not deal with Spector's personal life it is useful to point out some of the events which may have seriously affected him and his personal development, for example the fact that his father committed suicide when he was eight years of age. This could have had

a serious developmental effect on him. In the disturbed family situation that followed this suicide he found himself blamed for his father's suicide. This would have been a heavy burden of guilt for an eight-year-old to bear. Another event in his life was a very serious car accident in his later years. This left him for dead and he would have been pronounced dead if a medic at the scene had not detected the faintest of a pulse at the scene. This accident resulted in serious head injuries and a vast number of stitches in his head. It would appear that it may have left him brain damaged which may account for aspects of his very erratic behaviour subsequently.

Phil Spector was born on December 26, 1939 in The Bronx, New York, USA as Harvey Philip Spector. He is known for his work on Top Gun (1986), Dirty Dancing (1987) and Better Off Dead... (1985). He was married to Rachelle Marie Short , Janis Lynn Zavala, Ronnie Spector and Annette Lee Merar. He died on January 16, 2021 in San Joaquin County, California, USA.

Phil Spectre's song repetoir is so large that it would be impossible to list them all and this writer hopes to highlight some of them by means of providing a link for example one of the songs he co-wrote and is one of my favourites is 'Spanish Harlem":

https://www.youtube.com/watch?v=_LUdPaFRB60

The links which I provide will be largely from You Tube. It is for the reader to decide how he/she wishes to view or ignore aspects and content of these.

Here is a clip of Phil Spector " At home writing music"
https://www.youtube.com/watch?v=23y7pdefogM

Spector spoke of how he worked at menial tasks to repay the loan for a Corvette he purchased as a youth. This showed how he was prepared to work and succeed which was a trait which never left him. He became a millionaire in no time due to this quality which might be described as 'stickattedness' However it appears that he wanted the financial rewards for himself and was not into sharing the proceeds and would fight to have the financial profits for himself.

In this short story we rely heavily on what is in the public domain with links to You tube and other audio presentation. These are acknowledged. A major source was ***Wikipedia and Rolling Stones.*** The writer has to apologise for the advertisements that come with You Tube audios. The viewer can ignore the advertisements as he/she sees fit

Although much of his songs were produced in the early sixties, his versatility saw him working with a whole litany of stars. For example in the early 1970s, Spector produced the Beatles' *Let It Be* and several solo records by John Lennon and George Harrison. Analysis of Phil Spector and the Beatles 'Let it Be'

https://www.youtube.com/watch?v=wHddmBYyZKk

By the mid-1970s, Spector had produced eighteen US. Top 10 singles for various artists. His chart-toppers included the Righteous Brothers' "You've Lost That Lovin' Feelin'", the Beatles' "The Long and Winding Road", and Harrison's "My Sweet Lord". Following one-off productions for Leonard Cohen (*Death of a Ladies' Man*), Dion DiMucci (*Born to Be with You*), and the Ramones (*End of the Century*),

His honors include the 1973 Grammy Award for Album of the Year for co-producing Harrison's *Concert for Bangladesh*, a 1989 induction into the Rock and Roll Hall of Fame, and a 1997 induction into the Songwriters Hall of Fame.[11] In 2004,

Spector worked with Jerry Leiber and Mike Stoller and co-wrote the Ben E. King Top 10 hit "Spanish Harlem" with Jerry Leiber. Leiber and Stoller rec-ommended Spector to produce Ray Peterson's "Corrine, Corrine", which reached number 9 in January 1961. "He's a Rebel" was released on Philles, attributed to the Crystals, and quickly rose to the top of the charts.

In 1963 Spector released "Be My Baby" by the Ronettes, which went to number 2.   https://www.youtube.com/watch?v=0n81LW8WXk8

The Ronettes, 1966. Spector married front woman Veronica Bennett known as Ronnie, in 1968. In early 1965,Spector and Philles released "You've

Lost That Lovin' Feelin'" which became the label's second number 1 single. Other hits followed.   Spector, had a second number 1 hit in 1966 with the Bill Medley–produced "(You're My) Soul and Inspiration". The recording of   "Unchained Melody", was credited on some releases as a Spector production and Spector did have UK top 40 hits with the Ramones. Spector considered the single "River Deep – Mountain High" his best work, and Tina Turner was   successful   in Britain,   with   it   reaching   number 3.https://www.youtube.com/watch?v=e9Lehkou2Do

In early 1970, Allen Klein, the manager of the Beatles, involved Spector in several Beatles productions including John Lennon's solo single "Instant Karma!", which went to number 3, Spector was invited by Lennon and George Harrison to turn the Beatles' abandoned *Let It Be* recording sessions into a usable album. The reconditioned album topped the US. and UK charts. And resulted a number one US. single for "The Long and Winding Road"

For Harrison's multi-platinum album *All Things Must Pass* (number 1, 1970), Spector helped provide a symphonic ambiance *Rolling Stone*'s reviewer lauded the album's sound, calling it "Wagnerian, Brucknerian, the music of mountain tops and vast horizons". The triple LP yielded two major hits "My Sweet Lord" (number 1) and "What Is Life" (number 10). That same year, Spector co-produced Lennon's *Plastic Ono Band* (number 6) Spector co-produced Lennon's 1971 single "Power to the People" (number 11) and I*magine.*

Spector oversaw the live recording of the Harrison-organized Concert for Bangladesh shows in New York City, which resulted in the number 1 triple album *The Concert for Bangladesh*.

The album won the "Album of the Year" award at the 1973 Grammys. Spector said that the most creative period of his career was when he worked with Lennon and Harrison in the early 1970s. Lennon retained Spector for the 1971 Christmas single "Happy Xmas (War Is Over)"

In 1989, Tina Turner inducted Spector into the Rock and Roll Hall of Fame He was inducted into the Songwriters Hall of Fame in 1997 and he received the Grammy Trustees Award in 2000. Spector produced singer-songwriter Hargo Khalsa's track (known professionally as Hargo) "Crying for John Lennon", which originally appears on Hargo's 2006 album *In Your Eyes. On* a visit to Spector's mansion for an interview for the Lennon tribute film *Strawberry Fields*, Hargo played Spector the song and asked him to produce it.

Amy Winehouse referenced her admiration of Spector's work and often performed Spector's first hit song, "To Know Him Is to Love Him".

In mid-April 2008, BBC Two broadcast a special titled *Phil Spector: The agony and the ecstasy*, by Vikram Jayanti. In it he speaks about the musical instincts that led him to create some of his most enduring hit records, from "You've Lost That Lovin' Feelin'" to "River Deep, Mountain High" Spector himself is quoted as believing his production of Ike and Tina Turner's "River Deep, Mountain High" to be the summit of his Wall of Sound productions,[25] and this sentiment has been echoed by George Harrison, who called it "a perfect record from start to finish".

According to guitarist Stevie Van Zandt of the E Street Band, Spector was a "genius irredeemably conflicted". On Twitter, he wrote: "[Spector] was the ultimate example of the art always being better than the artist... [He] made some of the greatest records in history based on the salvation of love while remaining incapable of giving or receiving love his whole life."

Brian Wilson

Brian Wilson "Be My Baby", "Chapel of Love", "Just Once in My Life", "There's No Other (Like My Baby)", "Then He Kissed Me", "Talk to Me",

"Why Don't They Let Us Fall in Love", "You've Lost That Lovin' Feelin'",

"Da Doo Ron Ron",

https://www.youtube.com/watch?v=S-OTd7DXjlo I Can Hear Music", and

"This Could Be the Night".

THE WALL OF SOUND:

The Wall of Sound forms the foundation of Phil Spector's recordings.
The Wall of Sound is a music production formula developed by Phil Spector at Gold Star Studios, in the 1960s, with assistance from engineer Larry Levine and the conglomerate of session musicians later known as "the Wrecking Crew". The intention was to exploit the possibilities of studio recording to create an unusually dense orchestral aesthetic that came across well through radios and jukeboxes of the era. Spector explained in 1964: "I was looking for a sound, a sound so strong that if the material was not the greatest, the sound would carry the record. It was a case of augmenting, augmenting. It all fit together like a jigsaw." Songwriter Jeff Barry, who worked extensively with Spector, described the Wall of Sound as "by and large... a formula arrangement" with "four or five guitars ... two basses in fifths, with the same type of line ... strings ... six or seven horns adding the little punches ... and percussion instruments—the little bells, the shakers, the tambourines".

Bob B. Soxx & the Blue Jeans' version of "Zip-A-Dee-Doo-Dah" formed the basis of Spector and Levine's future mixing practices, almost never straying from the formula it established. For the recording of "You've Lost That Lovin' Feelin'", engineer Larry Levine described the process thus: they started by recording four acoustic guitars, playing eight bars over and over again, changing the figure if necessary until Spector thought it ready. They then added the pianos, of which there were three, and if they didn't work together, Spector started again with the guitars. This is followed by three basses, the horns (two trumpets, two trombones, and three saxophones), then finally the drums. The vocals were then added with Bill Medley and Bobby Hatfield singing into separate microphones and backing vocals supplied by the Blossoms and other singers.

Spector's wall of sound methodology is well explained in Wikipedia as follows:

Layering: source Wikipedia

The process was almost the same for most of Spector's recordings, with Spector starting by rehearsing the assembled musicians for several hours before recording. The backing track was performed live and recorded monaurally; a bass drum overdub on "Da Doo Ron Ron" was the exception to the rule.

Songwriter Jeff Barry, who worked extensively with Spector, described the Wall of Sound as "by and large ... a formula arrangement" with "four or five guitars ... two basses in fifths, with the same type of line ... strings ... six or seven horns adding the little punches ... percussion instruments—the little bells, the shakers, the tambourines".

Bob B. Soxx & the Blue Jeans' version of "Zip-A-Dee-Doo-Dah" formed the basis of Spector and Levine's future mixing practices, almost never straying from the formula it established. For the recording of "You've Lost That Lovin' Feelin'", engineer Larry Levine described the process thus: they started by recording four acoustic guitars, playing eight bars over and over again, changing the figure if necessary until Spector thought it ready. They then added the pianos, of which there were three, and if they didn't work together, Spector started again with the guitars. This is followed by three basses, the horns (two trumpets, two trombones, and three saxophones), then finally the drums. The vocals were then added with Bill Medley and Bobby Hatfield singing into separate microphones and backing vocals supplied by the Blossoms and other singers.

Daniel Lanois recounted a situation during the recording of the track "Good-bye" from Emmylou Harris's *Wrecking Ball*: "We put a huge amount of compression on the piano and the mandoguitar, and it turned into this fantastic, chimey harmonic instrument. We almost got the old Spector '60s sound, not by layering, but by really compressing what was already there between the melodic events happening between these two instruments." Nonetheless, layering identical instrumental parts remained an integral component of many of Spector's productions, as session musician Barney Kessel recalled:

> There was a lot of weight on each part... The three pianos were different, one electric, one not, one harpsichord, and they would all play the same thing and it would all be swimming around like it was all down a well. Musically, it was terribly simple, but the way he recorded and miked it, they'd diffuse it so that you couldn't pick any one instrument out. Techniques like distortion and echo were not new, but Phil came along and took these to make sounds that had not been used in the past. I thought it was ingenious.

All early Wall of Sound recordings were made with a three-track Ampex 350 tape recorder.] Levine explained that during mixing, "I [would] record the same thing on two of the [Ampex machine's] three tracks just to reinforce the sound, and then I would erase one of those and replace it with the voice. The console had a very limited equalizer for each input ... That was basically it in terms of effects, aside from the two echo chambers that were also there, of course, directly behind the control room."

Echo

Microphones in the recording studio captured the musicians' performance, which was then transmitted to an echo chamber—a basement room fitted with speakers and microphones. The signal from the studio was played through the speakers and reverberated throughout the room before being picked up by the microphones. The echo-laden sound was then channelled back to the control room, where it was recorded on tape. The natural reverberation and echo from the hard walls of the echo chamber gave Spector's productions their distinctive quality and resulted in a rich, complex sound that, when played on AM radio, had a texture rarely heard in musical recordings. Jeff Barry said: "Phil used his own formula for echo, and some overtone arrangements with the strings."

During the mixing for "Zip-A-Dee-Doo-Dah", Spector turned off the track designated for electric guitar (played on this occasion by Billy Strange). However, the sound of the guitar could still be heard spilling onto other microphones in the room, creating a ghostly ambiance that obscured the instrument. In reference to this nuance of the song's recording, music professor Albin Zak has written:

It was at this moment that the complex of relationships among all the layers and aspects of the sonic texture came together to bring the desired image into focus.

In order to offset the mixing problems percussion leakage caused, he applied a minimal number of microphones to the drum kits, using Neumann U67s overhead and RCA 77s on the kick to establish a feeling of presence.[3]

Wagnerian rock derives its characterization from a merge between Spector's Wall of Sound and the operas of Richard Wagner.

Spector's layered, symphonic "Wall of Sound" https://www.youtube.com/watch?v=kEEJZGATG9M can be seen in some of the recordings of Johnny Franz's mid-1960s productions for Dusty Springfield and the Walker Brothers as well as the Forum, a studio project of Les Baxter, Sonny Bono, a former associate of Spector, developed a variation on the Spector sound, which is heard mainly in mid-1960s productions for his then-wife Cher, notably "Bang Bang (My Baby Shot Me Down)".

Bruce Springsteen emulated the Wall of Sound technique in his recording of "Born to Run". Others influenced by Spector include George Morton, Sonny & Cher, the Rolling Stones, the Four Tops, Mark Wirtz, the Lov-in' Spoonful, and the Beatles. Swedish pop group ABBA cited Spector as an influence, and used similar Wall of Sound techniques in their early songs, including "Ring Ring", "Waterloo", and "Dancing Queen".The Los Angeles-based new wave band Wall of Voodoo takes their name from Spector's Wall of Sound.

Spector testified in a 2005 court deposition that he had been treated for bi-polar disorder ("manic depression") for eight years, saying, "No sleep, de-pression, mood changes, mood swings, hard to live with, hard to concentrate, just hard—a hard time getting through life, I've been called a genius and I think a genius is not there all the time and has borderline insanity."

Spector is one of a handful of producers to have number one records in three consecutive decades (1950s, 1960s and 1970s). Others in this group in-clude Quincy Jones (1960s, 1970s, and 1980s), George Martin (1960s, 1970s, 1980s, and 1990s), Michael Omartian (1970s, 1980s and 1990s), and Jimmy Jam and Terry Lewis (1980s, 1990s, and 2000s).

Awards and nominations

Year	Nominee / work	Award	Result
1972	George Harrison "My Sweet Lord"	Grammy Award for Record of the Year[96]	Nominated
1972	George Harrison *All Things Must Pass*	Grammy Award for Album of the Year[96]	Nominated
1973	George Harrison & Friends *The Concert for Bangladesh*	Grammy Award for Album of the Year[207]	Won
1989	Phil Spector	Rock and Roll Hall of Fame[94]	Inducted
1997	Phil Spector	Songwriter's Hall of Fame[11]	Inducted
2000	Phil Spector	Grammy Trustees Award[96]	Won

Publication	Country	Accolade	Year	Rank	Ref

Rolling Stone	US	Greatest Artists of All Time	2004, up-dated 2011	64	[20 8]
The Washington Times	US	Greatest Record Producers of All Time	2008	2	[20 9]

Phil Spector interview https://www.youtube.com/watch?v=f0w75JVXVow

Phil Spector LAST INTERVIEW CLIP and video   21 Feb 2020

https://www.youtube.com/watch?v=C6i9PJetUyg

This is a clip of the last interview that music producer Phil Spector has done. I am not sure who owns this clip I found it on another video platform and decided to upload it to YouTube. If you own this clip, please comment and let me know how I can reach you I really want to watch this whole interview and if you want me to remove it please tell me. Phillip Harvey Spector (born Harvey Phillip Spector, December 26, 1939) is an American record producer, musician, and songwriter who developed the Wall of Sound, a music pro-duction formula he described as a Wagnerian approach to rock and roll. Spector was dubbed the "First Tycoon of Teen" by writer Tom Wolfe and is acknowledged as one of the most influential figures in pop music history.

After the 1970s, Spector mostly retired from public life. In 2009, he was convicted of second-degree murder and has remained incarcerated since. Born in the Bronx, Spector began his career in 1958 as co-founder, guitarist, and vocalist of the Teddy Bears, penning their US number-one single "To Know Him Is to Love Him". In 1960, he co-founded Philles Records, and at the age of 21, became the youngest ever US label owner to that point. Over the next several years, he wrote, co-wrote, or produced records for acts such as the Ronettes and the Crystals, and later, John Lennon and George Harrison of the Beatles. He often employed what would become known as "the Wrecking Crew" as his de facto house band while collaborating with arranger Jack Nitzsche, engineer Larry Levine, and various Brill Building songwriters. Spector's other chart-topping singles include "You've Lost That Lovin' Feelin'" (co-written and produced for the Righteous Brothers, 1964), "The Long and Winding Road" (produced for the Beatles, 1970), and "My Sweet Lord" (produced for Harrison, 1970). Spector is considered the first auteur among musical artists for the unprecedented freedom and control he had over every phase of the recording process. Additionally, he helped engender the idea of the studio as an instrument, the integration of pop art aesthetics into music (art pop), and the art rock genre. His honors include the 1973 Grammy Award for Album of the Year for co-producing Harrison's

Concert for Bangladesh (1971), a 1989 induction into the Rock and Roll Hall of Fame, and a 1997 induction into the Songwriters Hall of Fame. In 2004, Rolling Stone magazine ranked Spector number 63 on their list of the "100 Greatest Artists of All Time". According to BMI, "You've Lost That Lovin' Feelin'" is the song that received the most US airplay in the 20th century.

Music in this video

Learn more

Listen ad-free with YouTube Premium

Song

Imagine

Artist

John Lennon

Album

Imagine

Writers

John Lennon

Licensed to YouTube by

UMG (on behalf of Virgin Records Ltd); UMPI, LatinAutorPerf, LatinAutor

- UMPG, CMRRA, Global Music Rights LLC, UNIAO BRASILEIRA DE

EDITORAS DE MUSICA - UBEM, IMPEL, and 12 music rights societies

Power To The People

Artist

John Lennon

Album

Power To The People

Writers

John Lennon

Licensed to YouTube by

UMG (on behalf of Calderstone-Beatles); Global Music Rights LLC, IM-

PEL, CMRRA, UMPI, EMI Music Publishing, LatinAutorPerf, LatinAutor

- UMPG, UNIAO BRASILEIRA DE EDITORAS DE MUSICA - UBEM,

and 11 music rights societies

Song

My Sweet Lord (2009 Mix)

Artist

George Harrison

Album

My Sweet Lord

Writers

George Harrison

Licensed to YouTube by

UMG (on behalf of Calderstone-Beatles); LatinAutor - PeerMusic, UNIAO

BRASILEIRA DE EDITORAS DE MUSICA - UBEM, CMRRA, Global

Music Rights LLC, SOLAR Music Rights Management, Concord Music

Publishing, LatinAutorPerf, and 13 music rights societies

Phil Spector Jukebox This is a link to a whole series of Phil Spector's com-

positions (short extracts so that the reader can experience the ambiance of

his musical compositions by means of links and reference.

 https://www.youtube.com/watch?v=-4MznjQgxHc

Brian Wilson tribute Brian says of Phil Spector 'He was it There was noth-

ing to compare He was everything"

https://www.youtube.com/watch?v=KiScLYNAoSc

Summary Highlights of Phil Spector's musical career source Rolling Stone

Phil Spector, Famed 'Wall of Sound' Producer Convicted of Murder, Dead at 81

Revolutionary producer behind some of pop music's most enduring songs dies from natural causes while serving prison sentence

By

KEITH HARRIS Source Rolling Stone

Michael Ochs Archives

Phil Spector, the monumentally influential music producer whose "Wall of Sound" style revolutionized the way rock music was recorded in the early 1960s,

Spector adopted what he famously referred to as "a Wagnerian approach to rock & roll," calling the hit records he assembled in the Sixties for artists like the Ronettes, the Crystals, Darlene Love and the Righteous Brothers "little symphonies for the kids." His productions were dense and orchestral, accumulating layer upon layer of guitars, horns, keyboards, strings and percussion, often with multiple instruments playing the same note in unison. His classic recordings relied on the brilliant contributions of a set of musicians dubbed the Wrecking Crew

"He's timeless," Brian Wilson said of Spector in 1966. "He makes a milestone whenever he goes into the studio and this has helped the Beach Boys evolve." Bruce Springsteen sought to recapture the grandeur of Spector's productions on *Born to Run.* " Springsteen said in his 2012 South by Southwest keynote speech. "And Phil's greatest lesson was sound. Sound is its own language."

https://www.youtube.com/watch?v=hS0hn3o0FnE

"A genius irredeemably conflicted, he was the ultimate example of the Art always being better than the Artist, having made some of the greatest records in history based on the salvation of love while remaining incapable of giving or receiving love his whole life," Stevie Van Zandt wrote on Twitter.

Harvey Philip Spector was born in the Bronx on December 26, 1939. His father died by suicide when Spector was nine years old. Spector moved to Los Angeles with his mother in 1953.

Spector took the title of his first production, "To Know Him Is to Love Him," from the inscription on his father's gravestone.

When he was 18, Spector caught the eye of veteran L.A. producer Lester Sill, who instructed Spector to go to New York and work with Sill's former proteges, the successful songwriters Jerry Leiber and Mike Stoller.

In late 1961, Spector and Sill formed Philles Records. Spector's reputation as a producer ballooned as he focused his attention on girl group the Crystals. Spector fired the original Crystals, replacing them with singer Darlene Love and her backing group, the Blossoms. The new Crystals' first single, the million-selling "He's a Rebel," became Philles' first Number One single. Just a year after forming the label, Spector bought out Lester Sill's share. At 21 years old, Phil Spector was a millionaire.

Spector expanded his trademark Wall of Sound even with help from the Wrecking Crew, which included Glen Campbell and Barney Kessel, pianist Leon Russell and drummer Hal Blaine – with Jack Nitzsche and Sonny Bono often arranging and overseeing the recordings. Spector created four Top 10 hits in 1963: the Crystals' "Da Doo Ron Ron" and "Then He Kissed

Me," Bob B. Soxx & the Blue Jeans' "Zip-a-Dee-Doo-Dah" and, greatest of all, the Ronettes' "Be My Baby,"

Spector had become rock & roll's first superstar producer – "the first tycoon of teen" as a 1964 Tom Wolfe profile famously dubbed him. The Righteous Brothers. "You've Lost That Lovin' Feeling" sold over 2 million copies and became Philles' third Number One hit.

 Spector produced John Lennon's solo hit "Instant Karma!" and was given the task of creating an album out of the group's abandoned *Get Back* sessions. The result was the Beatles final studio album, *Let It Be.* *https://www.youtube.com/watch?v=GvxW0vbKvsA*

George Harrison got Spector to produce his triple-album, *All Things Must Pass,* and John Lennon   co-produced *The Plastic Ono Band* and *Imagine, with him. And* his single "Happy Xmas (War Is Over)."

In 1974, Spector barely survived a car crash in Hollywood. He was thrown through the windshield of a car and nearly declared dead at the scene of the accident; it took hours of surgery to keep him alive – as well as more than 700 stitches in his head to his face and more than 400 to the back of his head.

Additional reporting by Daniel Kreps

Source: Rolling Stone

https://www.youtube.com/watch?v=jbp1h74-RUs

The Phil Spector Story by Derek Shelmerdine

 https://www.youtube.com/watch?v=u5JdlcxAkX4

"Phil Spector started out as a producer with Atlantic Records and produced the original Top Notes version of Twist and Shout. In late 1961 he set up the Philles label with Lester Sill. This ran until 1967 and it was here that he produced his legendary wall of sound singles with the Crystals, Ronettes, Darlene Love and the Righteous Brothers. The wall of sound era ended after Ike and Tina Turner's River Deep Mountain High single flopped in America. He went on the work with John Lennon and the Beatles and turned their Get Back master tapes into their final album, Let It Be. Spector also produced albums for Leonard Cohen and the Ramones. In 2009 he was convicted for the murder of actress Lana Clarkson".

The above is this writer's efforts to give the reader as complete a picture as he could of the writer producer musical genius Phil Spector's musical repertoire and creativity.

SUMMARY/ CONCLUSIONS:

Phil Spector was born on December 26, 1939 in The Bronx, New York, USA as Harvey Philip Spector. He grew up in The Bronx, NY, until age fourteen, when his family moved to Los Angeles. He is known for his work on Top Gun (1986), Mean Streets (1973) and Dirty Dancing (1987). He was married to Rachelle Marie Short , Janis Lynn Zavala, Ronnie Spector and Annette Lee Merar. He died on January 16, 2021 in San Joaquin County, California, USA.

Spector served an "apprenticeship" under Jerry Leiber and Mike Stoller in New York, learning from them while they were producing The Drifters; Spector plays the guitar solo at the end of "On Broadway".

His studio band was the 'Wrecking Crew'; session regulars included Hal Blaine, Glen Campbell, Al De Lory, Jim Gordon, Jim Horn, Carol Kaye, Leon Russell, Tommy Tedesco, Nino Tempo, and Sonny Bono. Brian Wilson sometimes "borrowed" Wrecking Crew members for his own recordings with The Beach Boys.

Spector was elected to the Rock and Roll Hall of Fame in 1989

Spector first met The Beatles in early 1964 and Allen Klein brought him to England, where he hit it off well and collaborated with John Lennon and **George Harrison**, and helped produce Lennon's solo single "Instant Karma!" Spector produced records for many artists including Gene Pitney, Ike Turner and Tina Turner, Ben E. King, The Beatles, **The Righteous Brothers**, The Checkmates, The Crystals, The Ronettes, Ramones and Yoko Ono, to name but a few. Spector was Inducted into the Songwriters Hall of Fame in 1997.

(1965) He played bass guitar on The Rolling Stones' single "Play With Fire".

- (1963) He played the guitar solo on The Drifters' recording of "On Broadway".

- (1961) Single: Produced "There's No Other Like My Baby" by The Crystals.

- (1962) Single: Produced "Second Hand Love" by Connie Francis.

- (1961) Single: Produced "Corinna, Corinna" by Ray Peterson.

- (1961) Single: Produced "Pretty Little Angel Eyes" by Curtis Lee.

- (1961) Single: Produced "I Love How You Love Me", by The Paris Sisters.

- (1961) Single: Produced "I'm So Happy" by The Ducanes. NOTE: This was a remake of the Frankie Lymon and the Teenagers song of the same name.

- (1961) Single: Produced "Under the Moon of Love" by Curtis Lee.

This writer finishes this short story with his favourite song which is called 'Imagine' and was a result of collaboration between John Lennon and Phil Spector. Here are the words of the song:

Imagine there's no heaven

It's easy if you try

No hell below us

Above us only sky

Imagine all the people

Living for today, I

Imagine there's no countries

It isn't hard to do

Nothing to kill or die for

And no religion too

Imagine all the people

Living life in peace

You may say I'm a dreamer

But I'm not the only one

I hope someday you'll join us

And the world will be as one

Imagine no possessions

I wonder if you can

No need for greed or hunger

A brotherhood of man

Imagine all the people

Sharing all the world, you

You may say I'm a dreamer

But I'm not the only one

I hope someday you'll join us

And the world will live as one

Source: Musixmatch

Songwriters: John Lennon

Imagine lyrics © Lenono Music, Kobalt Music Services Ltd Kms

https://www.youtube.com/watch?v=YkgkThdzX-8

POST SCRIPT

The purpose of this short story is to give the reader in so far as the present writer could, in a short story, the length and breath of Phil Spector's musical reach and content. It is not about Phil Spector the person. That aspect has been covered in countless articles and posts on the internet and elsewhere. It is for others to adjudicate with regard to his personality and psychology. Suffice it to say that he was a complex character full of genius and one of the most creative musical composers of the nineteenth century and more particularly the 1960s.

OBITUARY JAN. 19, 2021 – (extracts inferences and/conclusions) By Bill Wyman

"To Know Him Is to Love Him," by the Teddy Bears, was recorded when Spector was a 19-year-old and went to No. 1 on the national pop charts. Within a few years, Phil Spector was a cultural icon, a flamboyant impresario with an impressive string of hit singles. Spector was described by Tom Wolfe as "The First Tycoon of Teen"

His signature Wall of Sound consisted of one or two or three pianos, four or five or six guitars, as many bassists, drummers and percussionists, all playing together, precisely, and recorded with preternatural care to form a tsunami of aural effect. "Spector's real greatness is his ability to induce those incredible little moments of poignant longing in us," Leonard Cohen once reflected.

His highly volatile relationships with his mother and sister contributed to the darker side of his personality.

At the same time, he was a true musician. Many of those he worked with recall him as a man of unending energy, zany humor, and enthusiasm, able to keep a large corps of session musicians engaged while putting them through the gruelling processes that made his productions unique.

His character was characterised by meanness, the lack of affect when it came to the feelings of others; controlling approach to women, jealousies, and absence of sensitivity towards other's feelings

His father's suicide when Phil Spector was just eight years of age, left a broken and dysfunctional family behind. Phil Spector's parents were both from the families of Ukrainian immigrants. Phil Spector was born Harvey Philip Spector, on the day after Christmas, 1939, and grew up in the Bronx, at 1027 Manor Avenue. As a child, Spector was asthmatic, allergic to the sun, and dominated by an overprotective and utterly domineering mother.

Why his father committed suicide is unknown. One morning he headed off to his job in Brooklyn, parked, and then ran a hose from the exhaust pipe to the interior of his running car. His mother moved Harvey and his sister, Sharon, to Los Angeles. It was far from a happy family.

Phil was made to feel guilty over the death of his father. 'Your father killed himself because you were a bad child,'" a friend from high school is quoted in Mick Brown's definitive biography, _Tearing Down the Wall of Sound_. "And then he would say, 'Daddy killed himself because of you.' Your mother tells you this, you attack back with that. They would just attack each other all the time. There's a reason for everything, and with Phil the reason he's the way he is all to do with his immediate family." Mark Ribowsky's 1984 biography of Spector, _He's a Rebel_, begins with an epigraph from _Oedipus Rex_.

Spector had a fun and ingratiating side, when he chose to turn it on.

In December of 1958, "To Know Him Is to Love Him" became a No. 1 hit, a spot it held for three weeks, and eventually sold 1.4 million copies.

In Spector's early days there were no Beatles, Stones, or Motown. But innovative record men like Ahmet Ertegun and Jerry Wexler, of Atlantic Records, were bringing a new sophistication to pop with acts like Ruth Brown, the Coasters, and the Drifters and artists including Barry Mann and Cynthia Weil; Carole King and Gerry Goffin; Ellie Greenwich and Phil Barry; and Neil Sedaka and Howard Greenfield, part of the Brill Building song factory, and part of the company Aldon, co-owned by Don Kirshner, Pomus and Mort Shuman.

Phil Spector and Lester Sill christened their label Philles — i.e., "Phil" plus "Les," not "Phillies." This was the formal beginning of the Phil Spector era. (Spector quickly took full possession of the label.) He came back to Los Angeles and fixated on Gold Star, the small studio where he had crafted "To Know Him Is to Love Him." He began to assemble a corps of musicians who could help him achieve the increasingly ornate ambition he had for his next singles. Working with engineers Larry Levine and arranger Jack Nitzsche, he would work out of the tiny space and create more than a dozen top-40 hits.

The musicians were a large pool of session players, including guitarist Tommy Tedesco, <u>bassist Carol Kaye</u>, drummer Hal Blaine, and a few artists who went on to their own stardom such as keyboardist Leon Russell and guitarist Glen Campbell. They would play for Spector and then, as word of his productions got around, for people like Brian Wilson, who would adopt the studio and the players as his own and create the Beach Boys' most sprawling works there. As the pop industry grew and evolved, the same players would be gathered in various formations to play on countless other hits by many other hits over the next decade and beyond. While they had no formal name, in the future they would be called the Wrecking Crew.

His first distinctive touch was collecting that mass of instruments: guitarists, drummers, keyboardists and percussion players to start, and then sometimes strings and woodwinds in the mix as well. Where today individual drums in a drum set can be given their own track, back then the instruments were recorded en masse via microphones placed strategically around the (tiny and cramped) studio. (The vocals could be recorded separately.) Stereo was available, even in the early '60s, but all pop material was mixed back down to mono — a single track.

The players marveled as he would blend a piano and a harpsichord sound, for example, together until the instruments were indistinguishable. Spector discovered a makeshift echo room at Gold Star, a small space with concrete walls; he could route the sound into it, and then mic the sound back to the recording board. The sounds on Spector records would spur Wilson of the Beach Boys to great creativity as can be heard on Beach Boys works like "Good Vibrations" and the album *Pet Sounds*, and would in turn spur the competitiveness and creativity of the Beatles.

The Righteous Brothers, singers Bobby Hatfield and Bill Medley- Spector borrowed them from their label and created four massive hits for the pair in quick succession: first "You've Lost That Lovin' Feelin'," and then "Just Once in My Life," "Unchained Melody," and "Ebb Tide."

In January 1965 Spector was rewarded with a profile, "The First Tycoon of Teen," by Tom Wolfe, in the New York *Herald Tribune*, a highly prestigious paper (the progenitor of *New York*), and one that let people like Wolfe write in a highly impressionistic form. The piece began with Spector freaking out on an airplane taxiing for take-off and demanding that it be turned around so he could be let off. The event is portrayed a little bit more favorably toward the subject than the hysterical outburst warranted. Wolfe then dials things up to 11 and beyond:

"Every baroque period has a flowering genius who rises up as the most glorious expression of its style of life — in latter-day Rome, the Emperor

Commodus; in Renaissance Italy, Benvenuto Cellini; in late Augustan Eng-

land, the Earl of Chesterfield; in the sal volatile Victorian age, Dante Ga-

briel Rossetti; in late-fancy neo-Greek Federal America, Thomas Jefferson;

and in Teen America, Phil Spector is the bona-fide Genius of Teen."

The Beatles had recorded an album called *Get Back*, but it had not been released amid the then-bitter acrimony amongst the band members. Instead, Paul McCartney put the band through its paces for *Abbey Road*. The Beatles' manager, Allen Klein, from whom McCartney was estranged, offered the job of cleaning up the *Get Back* sessions for release to Spector.

His preparation of the album that would be released under the name *Let It Be* involved track selection, sequencing, and to some extent re-envisioning the songs on the tapes he was given by Klein. For three songs — "I Me Mine," "Across the Universe," and, most notoriously, Paul McCartney's "The Long and Winding Road" — Spector brought in a huge orchestral contingent, including nearly two dozen violins and violas, at an enormous cost. He also added what are invariably referred to as the "heavenly choirs," most glaringly on "Road." (Outside voices had never been heard on a Beatles record before.) It worked, in one sense: Spector could point out that the re-cast "Long and Winding Road" and the title song were No. 1 singles in the U.S., ending the band's career at a peak.

During this work, Spector established a relationship with John Lennon and George Harrison. He helped Lennon maneuver the studio and produce one of his most memorable solo singles, "Instant Karma." This beat-heavy chart, overlaid on one of the loudest of all the Wall of Sound productions, produced a No. 2 hit. Spector also produced George Harrison's epic and great-sounding *All Things Must Pass* album, Harrison's own artistic high point.

The gun incidents with Lennon weren't unusual. "I would say Hitlerian, the atmosphere was one of guns," Leonard Cohen, who shared a manager with Spector, later said. "I mean, that's what was really going on, guns. The music was subsidiary, an enterprise. People were armed to the teeth … you were slipping over bullets, and you were biting into revolvers in your hamburger. There were guns everywhere. "In 1980 Lennon was killed. In early 1991, Spector's song writing friend Doc Pomus died.

The events that led to the death of Clarkson in 2003 perhaps started that year. For unknown reasons, he and Zavalos split up; shortly afterward, one of their children, 9-year-old Phillip Spector Jr., died from leukemia. The child was the same age Spector had been when his father died. It was widely accepted among Spector's acquaintances that the death of his son left him bereft. "The most obscene and vile word in the language," Spector would say later, "is *dead.*"

John Haughton January 2022 short story about Phil Spector's creative music.

Buy your books fast and straightforward online - at one of world's fastest growing online book stores! Environmentally sound due to Print-on-Demand technologies.

Buy your books online at
www.morebooks.shop

Kaufen Sie Ihre Bücher schnell und unkompliziert online – auf einer der am schnellsten wachsenden Buchhandelsplattformen weltweit! Dank Print-On-Demand umwelt- und ressourcenschonend produziert.

Bücher schneller online kaufen
www.morebooks.shop

KS OmniScriptum Publishing
Brivibas gatve 197
LV-1039 Riga, Latvia
Telefax: +371 686 204 55

info@omniscriptum.com
www.omniscriptum.com